We Build a Birdhouse

By Alison Blank

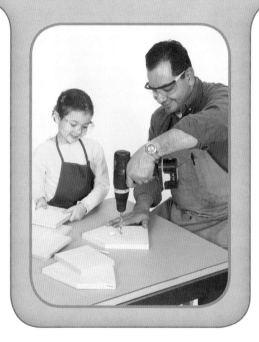

Scott Foresman
is an imprint of

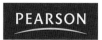

Glenview, Illinois • Boston, Massachusetts • Chandler, Arizona •
Upper Saddle River, New Jersey

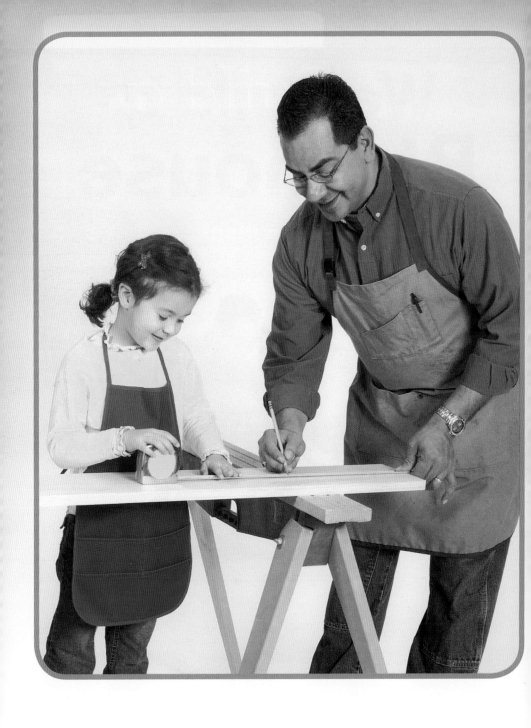

We measure.

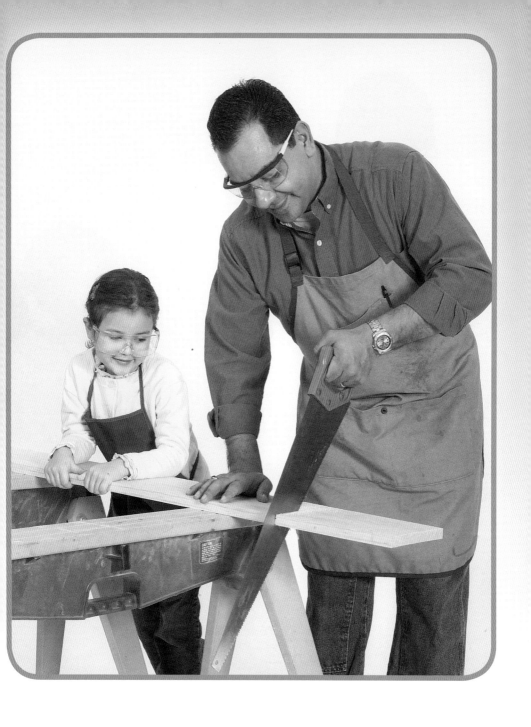

We saw.

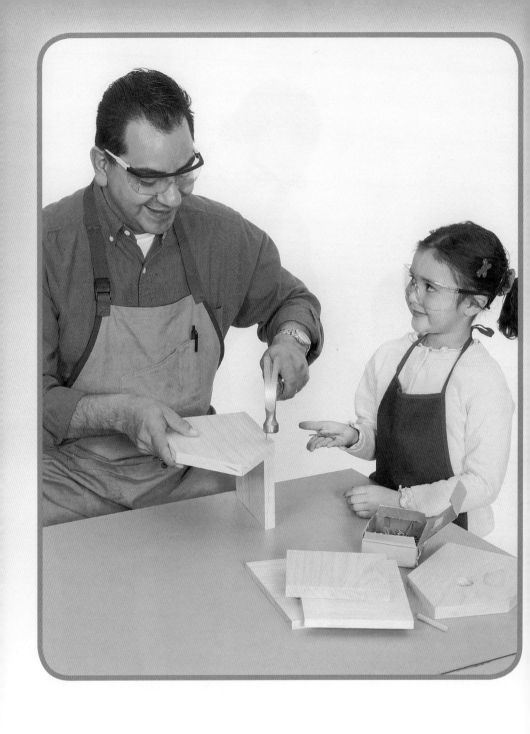

We hammer.

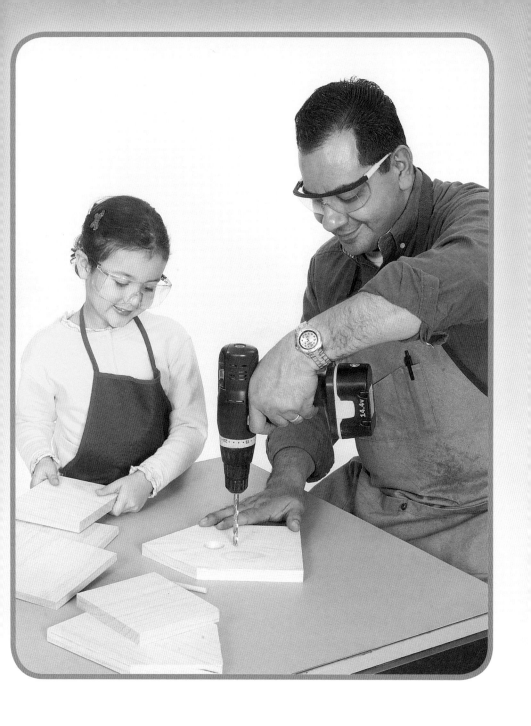

We drill.

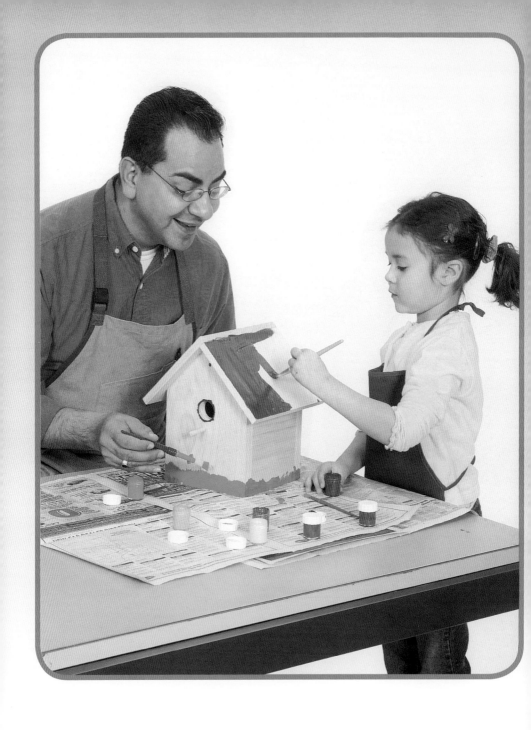

We paint.

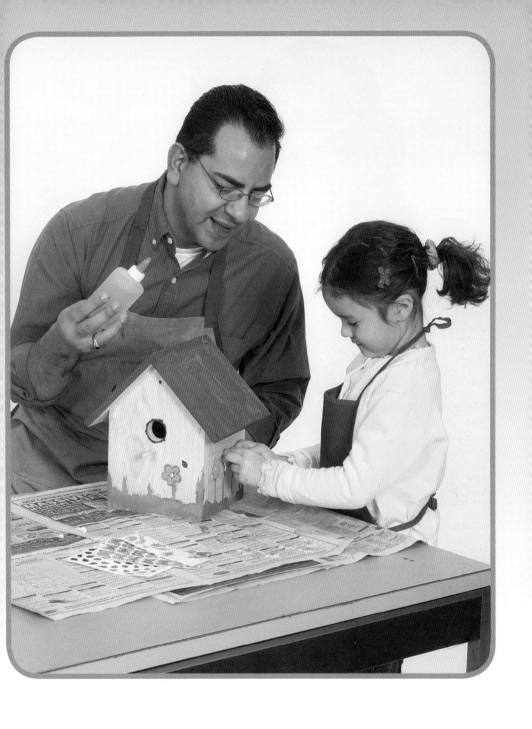

We glue.

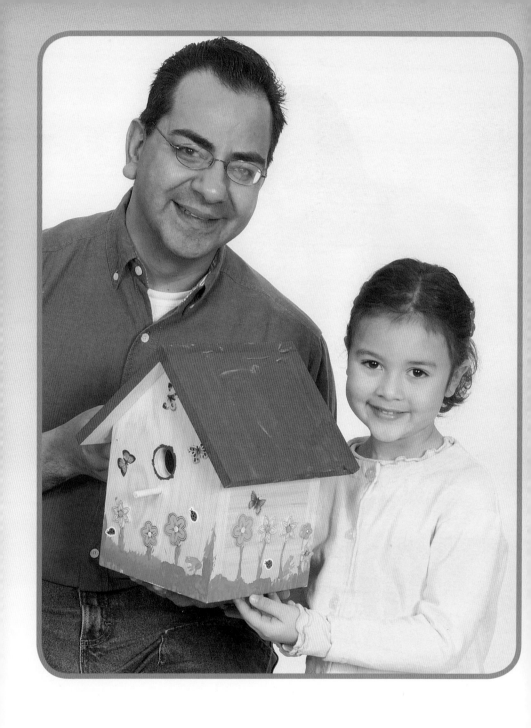

We build.